The Man Who Saved a Town:
Leo Norbury Murphy

A Biography

By Andrew Edwards

All proceeds from the sale of this book will be donated to the Royal British Legion.

**Dedicated to my good friend Ian McGowan RIP.
We walked many battlefields together.**

To Roy
with best wishes

Andrew Edwards

Contents

Foreword

Nine out of ten men who fought in World War 1 survived. This is the story of one of those men.

Andrew Edwards, September 2022

Introduction – My Journey

In April 1998, together with three friends, I travelled to Bethune in Northern France, our base for a weekend touring World War 1 (WW1) battlefields. On the Sunday morning I noticed the town hall was open and on venturing inside discovered, in the foyer, an exhibition covering WW1. On one of the walls in newspaper articles and photographs was featured one man, a British soldier, who had helped evacuate the town during a German bombardment in April 1918.

Upon returning home I tried to discover who the man was but drew a complete blank. Google searches of Bethune, evacuation, British soldier and so on, produced no results, however, the memory of seeing an Englishman remembered some 80 years on never left my thoughts.

In 2003, I was part of a work team which included a French national with the superb name of Cyril Le Roux. I recounted our trip to him and he offered to contact the town hall in Bethune seeking further information. The response was amazing. Not only did they provide a name (Leo Norbury Murphy), but also a short biography and a photograph of Leo pictured with the Mayor of Ypres and the Police Commissioner. It was the starting point.

Further Google searches produced very little. Accounts of the evacuation never mentioned the Englishman who had saved the town and who had been subsequently awarded the Croix de Guerre and Medal Militaire for his bravery.

In July 2018, the 100th anniversary of the ending of the Great War, I decided to revisit Leo's story. This time Google provided two hits. One was a Facebook post by historian Andrew Thornton, who specialises in documenting the history of The Old Contemptibles, with a short biography of Leo. The second hit was a set of documents held by The Surrey History Centre in Woking. Leo's eldest son, Francis, had originally deposited them with The Queen's Royal Surrey Regimental Museum. I contacted the centre, and they confirmed the documents were available and for a small fee could be copied and posted to me. Within a week I received a treasure trove – a short biography of Leo by his son Francis, copies of his Croix de Guerre and Medal Militaire citations, together with correspondence between Francis and the Queen's Royal Surrey Regimental Museum. The response from The Surrey History Centre in Woking was excellent, public service at its very best.

On the Facebook post concerning Leo by Andrew Thornton, was a comment from Susan Livings: "That's my grandad." I contacted Susan and explained I held several documents about her grandad, and so began a correspondence culminating in me sending her an initial draft of Leo's biography in March 2019.

Susan had told me of a cousin in Tasmania who was also interested in Leo's story, so when an airmail letter dropped through the post box from Cecilia Wootton in Tasmania, I opened it with excitement. Cecilia had shared a home with her mother, Andrée (Leo's daughter), and Leo's widow, Emelie. Cecilia recounts: "My memories of my early childhood days, say from 1950 onwards, was that the house became clogged up with stuff from the museum, in crate after crate after crate. We had to go sideways down the hallway. Mum got really cross with Grandma for not clearing it, but it was there for ages. Firstly, it had been in the building at the old Steine, corner of East

Street I think. I think the rent got too much, so they had to shift everything, and it ended up at my home in Loder Road, Preston Park, Brighton. Some bits were sold, but sadly there was little interest after WW2. I remember we had a short dagger to stir paint! It was a mid-green colour. My sister and I each had a German helmet in the attic, plumes, metal points, in very good condition, in large tins for protection. These disappeared in later years. I can't be sure, but I have a fair idea they were taken when Emelie died at Loder Road in 1977. Grandma finally agreed to get rid of it. She wanted to hang on to it, but we had nowhere to store it. These days it would be more appreciated."

I knew I had to do more, so I asked a French friend to contact the Bethune Town Council for help, much in the way that Cyril Le Roux had done sixteen years earlier. She was referred to the archivist, who had no information regarding Leo and referred us to the Ypres Museum.

I contacted the Ypres Museum by email explaining what I was trying to do and asking if they held any information on Leo. Later that day I received a reply from Museum Director, Dominiek Dendooven, with a one word opening sentence, "Obviously".

Dominiek went on to say, "As the founder of the predecessor of our museum, Murphy was a well-known figure and he is buried in our town cemetery. We hold a file on Murphy. There is more information in the master thesis Bert Heyvaert wrote on the British community in Ypres, and we hold photos of him and his museum, as well as some other items." It was time for me to head to Belgium!

I also received a lovely email from Professor Mark Connelly, co-author of *Ypres*, part of the Great Battle series. Mark provided encouragement and excellent advice on further sources of information.

It is now over 24 years since I first 'met' Leo in Bethune Town Hall, and as I discovered more and more about his life, I wanted to share his story. I hope you enjoy reading about the life of this remarkable man.

In the Beginning

Born in Manchester on 5th August 1891,[1] Leo Norbury Murphy was the son of William Henry Murphy, a music teacher, and Caroline Murphy née Norbury. Both parents were accomplished musicians and gave regular concerts in Manchester. Leo is recorded in the 1901 Census, aged nine, as residing with his parents and four brothers at 15 Fairfax Street in Scarborough.

Leo joined the 1st Battalion The Queen's (Royal West Surrey Regiment) in 1907, and in the 1911 Census is recorded as serving with the 1st Battalion at Warley Barracks. On completing his period of engagement with The Queen's, he was transferred to the Reserve.

---

[1]His birth was registered in the 3rd Quarter of 1891 (June/July/August) at Chorlton. Francis Murphy provided the actual DOB.

During the Great War

Great Britain declared war on Germany at 11:30pm on 4th August 1914. At 6am on 5th August (his 23rd birthday), Leo received his call up papers and was mobilised, re-joining the 1st Queens at Bordon Camp. Leo left Bordon camp at 8am the same morning, entrained for Southampton, eventually landing in France on 9th August 1914. Leo appears to have been attached to 1st Division Headquarters, the British Expeditionary Force.

The British Expeditionary Force

The British Expeditionary Force (BEF) was established by the Minister for War, Richard Haldane, after the Boer War. Its purpose was to enable the British Government to respond quickly to any crisis in the world that threatened British interests. The need for the force had been illustrated in the Boer War, as many of the soldiers involved had been ill-equipped and lacking in training for modern warfare. By the time that the First World War broke out, the BEF was a fighting force of approximately 100,000 men including Leo and 1,000 men of The 1st Battalion, The Queen's Royal West Surrey Regiment. The BEF, whilst small compared to the armies of France and Germany, consisted of highly trained and battle-hardened soldiers.

Belgium

When Germany invaded Belgium on 4th August 1914, the BEF was sent to France to help to halt the German advance. It was first engaged in combat at the Battle of Mons, at which it was heavily outnumbered and forced to retreat. The BEF, alongside French troops, were more successful at the Battle of the Marne, where the German advance through Belgium and eastern France was curtailed by a decisive Allied victory. Here, the German forces were pushed back over the River Aisne, preventing the capture of Paris.

After the Battle of the Marne in late September 1914, the so-called 'Race to the Sea' began, as each army attempted to outflank the other on their way northwards, hastily constructing trench fortifications as they went. The race ended in mid-October at Ypres, the ancient Flemish city with its fortifications guarding the ports of the English Channel and access to the North Sea beyond. Leo and his regiment fought in both the Battle of the Marne and the Battle of the Aisne.

The first battle of Ypres

On 19th October, near the Belgian city of Ypres, a protracted period of fierce combat began. The Germans opened their Flanders offensive and the Allies steadfastly resisted, while seeking their own chances to go on the attack wherever possible. Fighting continued, with heavy losses on both sides, until 'The Critical Day', 31st October 1914, and the Battle of Gheluvelt.

The Battle of Gheluvelt

The Kaiser had proclaimed his intention to join his forces for a triumphant entry into Ypres and the small village of Gheluvelt on the Ypres to Menin Road stood in the way of the advancing German army. The remnants of several British battalions who had been fighting day and night to guard the road faced overwhelming odds against the well-equipped German army. An artillery bombardment began as daylight broke and the German infantry attacked. Many of the British units were decimated. One of these, Leo's 1st battalion of The Queen's Surrey Regiment, faced a German attack from their front and was enfiladed from either flank, trapped and unable to move. When all seemed lost, the order was given for the 357 men of the Worcester Regiment to attack. The Worcester's had been held in reserve in nearby Polygon Wood overlooking the town. They ran at the double, over open ground for a thousand yards ignoring the German machine guns and artillery shells exploding above and around them. Wounded men on the battlefield cried out to them to go back as certain death awaited them. Over 100 men of The Worcester's were killed during the charge. The Germans were taken by surprise and were either killed or retreated, leaving weapons and equipment in their wake.

At roll call after the battle, Leo was one of only 32 survivors out of nearly 1000 men in his Battalion who had set out from England in August. This number included cooks and transport.[2]

Overall, in the first battle of Ypres, the allies suffered 20,000 casualties and the Germans around 13,500.

---

[2]Page 139 *The Battle Book of Ypres* by Beatrix Brice. Published in 1927. Historian Andrew Thornton advised me these roll calls are often inaccurate with wounded and disorientated soldiers turning up later.

"October 31st and November 1st will remain forever memorable in the history of our country, for, during those two days, no more than one thin and straggling line of tired-out British soldiers stood between the Empire and its practical ruin as an independent first-class Power." (General John French, 1914)[3]

Gheluvelt Chateau was completely destroyed during the battle, but was beautifully restored after the war by its owner, Leonie Keingiaert. Born into an aristocratic family in Leuven, she was elected Mayor of Gheluvelt, in October 1921, after a law was passed the previous August allowing women to serve as mayors. Leonie founded a brickyard not only to restore her chateau, but also to rebuild houses for returning refugees. Her chateau was not completed until 1929, with priority given to building houses for the local population.

Gheluvelt Park, in Worcester, England, was opened on 17th June 1922 by (the now) Field Marshal John French, 1st Earl of Ypres, to commemorate the Worcestershire Regiment's part in the Battle of Gheluvelt. General French stated during the opening ceremony, "On that day the 2nd Worcesters saved the British Empire.[4]"

In Leo's own words, when the Battle of the Somme became 'interesting', he fought in and survived that battle.

Leo was transferred to the 10B Battalion, The Royal Fusiliers in 1916 and employed on military intelligence tasks. He was issued with the regimental

---

[3]The book *1914* by Viscount French of Ypres.
[4]*Gheluvelt Park*, Wikipedia.

number L/17727 and appointed an Acting Corporal.

Béthune

During the war, Béthune was mostly defended by British forces, but included units of the Canadian and Indian armies, and initially suffered little damage. It was an important railway junction and hospital site, holding the 33rd Casualty Station until December 1917.

In the spring of 1918, the German High Command decided to carry out a series of attacks at various places along the Western Front and this became known as the Spring Offensive. The Germans had realised that their only remaining chance of victory was to defeat the Allies before the overwhelming human and material resources of the United States could be fully deployed. In Flanders, an attack along the Lys River enabled the German Army to take Bailleul and threaten Mount Kemmel. However, once again, they failed at Béthune.

This failure provoked the Germans into bombarding the town centre with incendiary and shrapnel shells. Béthune burned for more than four days, and the main square and its surrounding buildings were completely destroyed. The sandstone bell tower, which dated from the 15th century, was damaged, but remained standing thanks to the protection afforded to it by the surrounding buildings. The town hall and many other buildings were seriously damaged. Named sub-prefect on 12th January 1914, Adrien Bonnefoy-Sibour carried out his duties with courage and composure throughout the war. However, by 12th April 1918, the situation had deteriorated to such an extent that the order was given

15

to evacuate Béthune, although the sub-prefect and 50 diehards remained.[5]

Leo, through his role with Military Intelligence, realised the town of Béthune which had largely escaped bombardment during the war, would be heavily shelled. On 13th and 14th April, he organised the evacuation of the population, via train, during the bombardment. Whilst moving through the town, with artillery shells falling all around, Leo heard cries coming from a bombed-out building. He dug down and found Ernest and Arméline Droy, together with their daughter Emélie, covered in rubble, in the building's cellar. Once safely extracted they were evacuated on the next train.

On 28th December 1919, Adrien Bonnefoy-Sibour received French president Raymond Poincaré, who awarded Béthune the Legion of Honour and the Military Cross.

After the war, public money earmarked for reconstruction was mostly spent on the main square and private initiatives were relied upon to rebuild the rest of the town. Because of the narrowness of the plots of land (often less than 2.7 metres in front of the buildings), the architect in charge of the renovation works, Jacques Alleman, chose to give the facades high gables with ornamental reliefs combining Art Deco and regionalist styles. He used the same architectural solutions for the new town hall, but adapted them to the monumental character of the building. The town hall's facade shows the Béthune coat of arms surrounded by the military honours it received in the aftermath of the war.[6]

---

[5]*Bethune and the British* – Northern France Tourist Board.
[6]*Bethune and the British* – Northern France Tourist Board.

Bravery Awards

Leo was awarded the Medaille Militaire and the Croix de Guerre with bronze star by the French Government for his part in organising the evacuation of civilians from Bethune in April 1918. The announcement that he had been awarded the Medaille Militaire was published in *The London Gazette* on 8th October 1918, and that for the Croix de Guerre was gazetted on 7th January 1919. Both award announcements gave his home address as Holland Park in West London.

Béthune Today

Béthune is a beautiful town, rich in architectural heritage and history. It has, amongst other features, a large, paved square with shops, cafés and a 47-metre-tall belfry standing in the centre from the top of which the Belgian border can be seen. The Carillon in the belfry is composed of 36 bells. The current belfry plays melodies every 15 minutes, including the children's lullaby, 'my little darling'. The belfry survived the fighting, albeit severely cracked and its top section missing. It is the last remaining building of the medieval period in Béthune, dating from 1386 and would have been completely flattened, but for the protection of the houses that surrounded it. Initially the idea was to leave it in ruins as a reminder of German barbarity. Restoration works officially ended on 6th October 1929 with the inauguration of the new chimes. The tenor bell bears the inscription: *'VIGILANT IS MY NAME. I replace Joyful who was destroyed by war, and from the top of this restored belfry, I ring for Peace and to the glory and the future of Béthune rebuilt.[7]'*

---

[7]*Bethune and the British* – Northern France Tourist Board.

After the First World War

Following his demobilisation in 1919, Leo returned to Béthune where he met with the Droy family who he had rescued from the cellar of their bombed house. Romance was in the air and Leo began a courtship with Emélie, the daughter, leading to their wedding later that year. Leo was later to recount how he was 'introduced' to his wife, a Frenchwoman, when she was covered by bricks and fallen masonry, and, in his own words they "lived happily ever after".

Leo and Emélie went on to have three (surviving) children: two sons and one daughter. Leo and his wife moved to Vlamertinghe, Belgium in 1921 and soon set up several businesses, most notably the British Touring and Information Bureau based in the Ypres Boomgaardstraat, providing guided tours around the battlefields of the Ypres Salient.

Veterans, widows and relatives would depart from Victoria Station in London by train to Dover. From Dover they would take the ferry to Ostend where Leo would meet them with a fleet of luxury coaches. They would then commence an organised tour of the WW1 battlefields in France, Holland and Belgium, with hotel and transport provided. Leo also established the Ypres Salient Museum in the old meat market in the centre of Ypres, whilst Emélie opened a handmade lace shop opposite. Visitors to the museum would be 'guided' over to the lace shop once they had finished viewing the museum exhibits! Leo spoke six languages and was a Fellow of the Institute of Linguists.

Visitors included veterans from the defeated German army. Leo recalled one visitor in particular in the summer of 1929, General Otto Von Hugel, who was in charge of the German forces in the salient from 1914 to 1916. Leo told one writer: "They even try to engage me in conversation about the rights and wrongs of the War. Old General von Hugel, who loosed off the first gas attack against Ypres, was down here for quite an hour the other day blathering away. Then he sailed off to attend the unveiling of our 20th Division Memorial at Langemarc. Utterly impenitent, the whole bunch of them, sign the visitors' book with a flourish, but I've got a special one for them[8]." Leo himself was gassed twice during the war and suffered breathing problems as a result for the rest of his life

The Old Contemptibles

To be an 'Old Contemptible' was to be part of an exclusive fellowship, forged by fire and blood during the first months of the Great War in 1914. The story of how the epithet came to be adopted by the men who served with the British Expeditionary Force during the early fighting is well known. Emperor Wilhelm II of Germany, who was famously dismissive of the British Expeditionary Force, allegedly issued an order on 19th August 1914 to, "Exterminate the treacherous English and walk over General French's contemptible little army[9]." Hence, in later years, the survivors of the BEF dubbed themselves 'The Old Contemptibles'. They referred to each other as 'chums' and the men who bore the

---

[8]*The Sphere* – 23 July 1927: An extract from an article by Ferdinand Tuohy entitled "Forever England... Today amidst the ruins of the Salient".
[9]No evidence of any such order being issued by the *Kaiser* has ever been found.

nickname were regarded as being of a particularly special quality.

As the war continued, and their ranks thinned, a soldier who had been 'out since Mons' was often held with a similar high regard by his less-experienced comrades as the 'Waterloo Men' of a century before. This distinction was more formally marked in November 1917, when the 1914 Star was instituted. The qualification date for the medal was those who had served with the British Expeditionary Force in France and Belgium between 5th August and midnight of 22nd November 1914.

In October 1919, a 'clasp' – in reality a bar to be sewn onto the ribbon of the medal – and two silver rosettes, to be borne on the medal ribbon bar for occasions when orders and decorations were not worn, were authorised. Eligibility for the 'clasp and roses' was determined by the qualification that individuals had "served under fire or who had operated within range of enemy mobile artillery in France or Belgium during the period between 5th August and 22nd November 1914." The devices were not automatically issued, but had to be applied for and the criteria of qualification had to be verified before they were sent out. Those men (and several women) who wore the 1914 Star and clasp were considered to be true 'Old Contemptibles' by their peers.[10]

Leo served as President of the Ypres Branch of The Old Contemptibles' Association and also joined the Ypres Branch of the British Legion on its formation.

When the tourist season closed, during the winter months, Leo worked as an electrician and sold

---

[10]Andrew Thornton, Military historian and author.

appliances from his premises on the Grand Place, advertising his services in the local Flemish newspapers.

Remembrance

The people of Béthune never forgot the Englishman who had helped to save them from certain death. Leo often revisited the town after the war, welcomed as the hero he was. In 1932 he was invited by the Mayor of Westminster (London) to participate in the Armistice ceremony at the Cenotaph on 11th November that same year. The journey by ship from Ostend to Dover and then Pullman train to London Victoria station was escorted by the Royal Airforce. On the Armistice Eve, the Bishop of Willesden said in St Martins in the Fields Church, "Anyone visiting the Ypres Salient War Museum will go forth and forever preach peace amongst nations[11]."

---

[11]*Leeds Mercury* – 11 March 1935.

World War 2

Following the outbreak of World War Two (WW2), Leo was advised by the British Embassy that the invading Germans would learn he had served in the Intelligence corps and the family could therefore be expected to be deported as slave labour to Germany. The family fled to England with just a suitcase each. Leo's son Francis recalled they were met by a reception committee in Dover and told:

"Welcome to the UK, we are here to help the people escaping; we have a small amount of pocket money and a list of accommodation and suitable jobs. Now are you Dutch?"
"No."
"Are you Belgian?"
"No."
"Well, you must be French?"
"No, we are British."
"Oh sorry! We've got nothing for you. We're here to help the foreigners[12]."

Leo had already managed to move part of his collection to England and in 1940 established a new museum at Gloucester Place in Brighton, charging an admission of 1s. for adults, 6d. for children, and half-price entry to members of the armed forces. What remained of the collection in Ypres disappeared during the German occupation. In Brighton, Leo and his collection were not successful: the authorities

---

[12]Francis Murphy in an interview with Sue Elliot for the book, *The Children Who Fought Hitler*.

requisitioned the building where he had installed his war exhibition and the collection was stored in a warehouse and in his daughter Andrée's small terraced house, never to be exhibited again. Leo was subsequently declared bankrupt. However, as this entry in the London Gazette confirms, he was soon back on his feet.

THE LONDON GAZETTE, 11 MAY, 1943

ORDER OF DISCHARGE.

No. 21. MURPHY, Leo Norbury, 41, Rugby Road, Brighton, Sussex, CURATOR of the International War Exhibition, at Nos. i to 4, Gloucester Place, Brighton. Date of Order of Discharge— May 6, 1943. Court—BRIGHTON and LEWES (at Brighton).
No. of Matter—
Y-46.

After the Second World War

In 1946, Leo and his family returned to Belgium following the end of WW2, only to find his house had been occupied by a former neighbour who informed him that under Belgian law he had to give one year's notice before the family could move back in! All the furniture had been removed – the piano was found in the town theatre, a leather armchair in the mayor's office and two large baskets of lace in the town hall. Leo was unable to re-start his museum as there was little interest in WW1 following the events of 1939-1945. Instead, Leo and his wife Emélie established a business selling lace and pinwork.

Leo died on 21st August 1951 of a heart attack following a year of heart problems. His daughter, Andrée, remembers, "He felt tired, went to bed and that was that." His death was reported in Het Ypersch Nieuws on 25th August. He was buried in Ypres Town Cemetery, near Row A3 of the Commonwealth War Graves Commission plot, his headstone set at a right-angle to the military graves. His effects, valued at £95 7s. 9d. were left to his widow Emélie Rose Murphy, probate being granted at Lewes on 28th November 1951.

Leo's life's work would only survive the man by a few years: the final end of the Ypres Salient War Museum came in 1954 when his widow Emélie, most regretfully, after exhausting every avenue open to her, sold the stored collection in Brighton as junk. Thousands of helmets, grenades, trench signs and other war equipment were melted. A journalist of *The Brighton Evening Argus* explained that the steel would be re-used in the British car industry and wrote without irony: "So you may soon have a scrap of history in your new motor car." The quote is typical of the attitude to WWI heritage at the time.

Following Leo's death, Emélie returned to England and became a nanny for wealthy families in London who were eager for their offspring to become fluent French speakers. In between assignments she lived with her daughter, Andrée, and Andrée's two daughters, Cecilia and Barbara, in Loder Road, Brighton.

Leo was a man of many parts, Soldier, Spy, Survivor, Hero, Entrepreneur, certainly a larger than life character.

As I reflect on Leo's life and achievements, one of his greatest accomplishments was to chaperone the relatives and family of those lost in the Great War to say a final farewell to their loved ones. Many war graves carry poignant messages from loved ones such as the one on Private R. Christopher's gravestone, who also served with Leo's regiment, The Queen's. He was killed on 6th April 1916 and is buried in Bethune cemetery. '*In memory of Robert my husband who loved me and gave himself for me*'. Leo helped to provide grieving relatives with some form of closure following the death of their loved ones.

In Leo's Footsteps

I contacted Dominiek and made arrangements to view Leo's file on Tuesday, 10th September. I set off for Ypres from Dover on Monday, 9th September. After arriving at my hotel in Ypres, I made my way to the Menin Gate Memorial.

Leo joined the Ypres branch of the British Legion on its formation, and also served as President of the Ypres Branch of The Old Contemptibles' Association. He often attended the Last Post ceremony, both as a participant laying wreaths, and as an observer.

The memorial is dedicated to the British and Commonwealth soldiers who were killed in the Ypres Salient during WW1, whose graves are unknown. The memorial is located at the eastern exit of the town and marks the starting point for one of the main roads out of the town that led Allied soldiers to the front line. Designed by Sir Reginald Blomfield and built by the Imperial War Graves Commission (it has since been renamed the Commonwealth War Graves Commission), the Menin Gate Memorial was unveiled on 24th July 1927.

Its large Hall of Memory contains the names, on stone panels, of 54,395 Commonwealth soldiers who died in the Salient, but whose bodies have never been identified or found. On completion of the memorial, it was discovered to be too small to contain all the names as originally planned. An arbitrary cut-off point of 15th August 1917 was chosen and the names of 34,984 UK soldiers still missing after this date were inscribed on the Tyne Cot Memorial to the Missing instead.

The Menin Gate Memorial does not list the names of the missing New Zealand and Newfoundland soldiers, who are instead honoured on separate memorials. To this day, the remains of missing soldiers are still found in the countryside around the town of Ypres. Typically, such finds are made during building work or road-mending activities. Any human remains discovered receive a proper burial in one of the war cemeteries in the region. If the remains can be identified, the relevant name is removed from the Menin Gate.

Following the Menin Gate Memorial opening in 1927, the citizens of Ypres wanted to express their gratitude towards those who had given their lives for Belgium's freedom. Hence, every evening at 8:00pm, buglers from the Last Post Association close the road which passes under the memorial and sound the 'Last Post'. Except for the occupation by the Germans in WW2, when the daily ceremony was conducted at Brookwood Military Cemetery in Surrey, England, this ceremony has carried on uninterrupted since 2nd July 1928. On the evening that Polish forces liberated Ypres in the Second World War, the ceremony was resumed at the Menin Gate, despite the fact that heavy fighting was still taking place in other parts of the town.[13]

I was privileged to witness the ceremony in person for both days I stayed in Ypres, accompanied by hundreds of people, both visitors and locals.

On the Tuesday morning I made my way to the In Flanders Fields Museum reading room. Dominiek was waiting for me and had Leo's file ready. Much of the file had been left previously by Cecilia and copies

[13] *Menin Gate,* Wikipedia & In Flanders Field Museum

were already in my possession, however, there were two special items. The first was a transcript of an interview with Leo's son, Francis, by author Sue Elliot, who co-wrote *The Children who fought Hitler*. The second was a Welsh bible authenticated as part of Leo's museum collection, and the only known museum item left in existence.

After a morning spent reading Leo's file I took a tour of the (very modern!) In Flanders Field Museum. The museum has many interactive displays and I suspect appeals to a younger audience in this digital age.

With instruction from Dominiek on the exact location of Leo's grave, I set off for the town cemetery, collecting some poppies on the way to leave on behalf of Susan and Cecilia. It was a strange moment as I approached Leo's grave, and although I'm not a religious person, I did say a few words to the man whose life had led me there.

As I walked to the grave I passed a military history shop offering guided tours of the Ypres Salient, so on my return journey I booked myself on a tour of the North part of the Ypres Salient. On the Wednesday morning at 10:00am we met outside the shop and were greeted by a young lady from Liverpool, who proved to be a brilliant guide.

First stop was Essex farm cemetery, the site of a British Advanced Dressing Station (A.D.S.). It is believed to be the place in May 1915 where the Canadian army doctor and artillery brigade commander, Major John McCrae, composed his famous poem, *In Flanders Fields*.

The red poppies growing in the warm spring weather amongst the military graves near to the makeshift medical bunker where John McCrae was working during that time, are believed to have been the inspiration for the poem. The symbol of the red poppy and the death of a friend, Lieutenant Alexis Helmer, deeply affected McCrae during the time of his involvement in the Second Battle of Ypres.

Opposite John Macrae's memorial our guide recited, word perfect, his beautiful poem: *In Flanders Fields*.

In Flanders fields the poppies blow
Between the crosses, row on row,
That mark our place; and in the sky
The larks, still bravely singing, fly
Scarce heard amid the guns below.
We are the dead, short days ago
We lived, felt dawn, saw sunset glow,
Loved and were loved, and now we lie
In Flanders fields.

Take up our quarrel with the foe:
To you from failing hands we throw
The torch; be yours to hold it high.
If ye break faith with us who die
We shall not sleep, though poppies grow
In Flanders fields.

I noticed several headstones placed next to each other rather than spaced out. Our guide informed us that these are known as shoulder to shoulder graves, where men had died alongside each other in a single incident, usually as a result of artillery fire.

Also in Essex farm lies the grave of rifleman Valentine Joe Strudwick, Service Number 5750, who served with 8th Battalion The Rifle Brigade. Valentine was aged just 15 when he died on 14th

January 1916. He is one of the youngest British casualties of the Great War to die in action.

Our next stop was the German war cemetery of Langemark near the village of the same name. More than 44,000 soldiers are buried here. The village was the scene of the first gas attacks by the German army on the Western Front, the beginning of the Second Battle of Ypres in April 1915, and which Leo referred to in one of his talks to visitors.

Located near the entrance is a mass grave known as the comrades' grave, containing the remains of 24,917 servicemen. Between the oak trees, next to this mass grave, are another 10,143 soldiers (including two British soldiers killed in 1918). At the front of the cemetery is a sculpture of four mourning figures by Professor Emil Krieger. The group was added in 1956 and is said to stand guard over the fallen.

I noticed one of the names on the memorial wall stood out from being touched and rubbed by visitors over the years. The name was Werner Voss, a fighter ace with 47 confirmed victories, second only to the Red Baron, Manfred von Richthofen. Werner was shot down and killed after engaging in a dogfight with six British fighters.

Also hanging on the panel was a tribute to one of two British soldiers buried here, Private Leonard Lockley, from his nephew and great niece.

Next we visited the site of the first German gas attacks of the war. At a location known as Vancouver Corner, which is about a mile south-east of Langemark where Zonnebekestraat meets the N313, is the Canadian 'Brooding Soldier' Memorial. It was near the village of Langemark on the 22nd April 1915 that the Germans first used poison gas. They advanced around two miles towards Ypres following this use of gas. Leo bitterly referred to this gas attack in his conversations with visiting journalists to his museum. Canadian troops were among those affected badly by the gas, and around 2000 Canadians died in this attack.

Our final stop was Tyne Cot Cemetery, the largest Commonwealth War Graves Commission cemetery in the world. It is now the resting place of more than 11,900 servicemen of the British Empire from WW1.

The stone wall surrounding the cemetery makes-up the 'Tyne Cot Memorial to the Missing', one of several Commonwealth War Graves Commission Memorials to the 'Missing' along the Western Front and whose graves are known only unto God".

The memorial contains the names of 33,783 soldiers from the UK forces, plus a further 1,176 New Zealanders. Three British Army Victoria Cross recipients are commemorated here.

It was an enjoyable tour, which I can highly recommend. The tour can be booked at The British Grenadiers Bookshop just a few yards from the Menin Gate.

Time to pick up Leo's trail again and onto the village of Gheluvelt, the site of the Battle of Gheluvelt. I parked by the lovely church and made my way to the two memorials – one to the South Wales Borderers and the second to the Worcestershire Regiment. They are located at the end of a pedestrian cul-de-sac and positioned against an incongruous backdrop of some farm buildings.

It was now time to travel to Bethune, the town where all those years ago I first came across Leo and began my journey. As I drove towards the town centre the belfry suddenly came into view and I felt a surge of adrenalin, similar to the experience of meeting an old friend after many years.

First thing next morning I made a visit to the beautiful church of Saint Vaast with its stunning stained glass windows and a memorial to the British Commonwealth war dead.

There are several war memorials in Bethune for WW2. Bethune was occupied by the Germans (unlike during WW1) from May 1940 until 4th September 1944, when the British, together with local resistance fighters, liberated the town. In memory, in 1947, a square was renamed Place du 4 Septembre 1944.

The town's citizens suffered greatly under occupation. Food rationing was introduced, and they faced deportations, arbitrary executions, and bombing.

Time now to visit the railway station and the scene of the population fleeing, via trains, in April 1918 whilst the town was under bombardment. Nowadays Bethune is a modern station and a hub in the French transport network, enabling travellers to reach all parts of France and the wider continent.

My final destination in Bethune was the town cemetery which, beyond the grand civilian graves, contains a section for the British war dead. Here I witnessed the great work carried out by the Commonwealth War Graves Commission maintaining the grounds and graves to the highest standard.

As I walked among the graves I was struck by how many carry the inscription 'Known unto God'. This phrase is used on the gravestones of unknown soldiers in Commonwealth War Graves Commission cemeteries. The phrase was selected by British poet Rudyard Kipling, who worked for what was then the Imperial War Graves Commission during the First World War.

Other graves carry poignant, personal messages from family members, and I reflected on the importance of Leo's work, bringing people to visit the last resting place of their fallen loved ones and maybe bringing some solace.

Photo Gallery

All photographs are shared with kind permission of the copyright owners.

The Murphy family in 1906 with young Leo on the right.

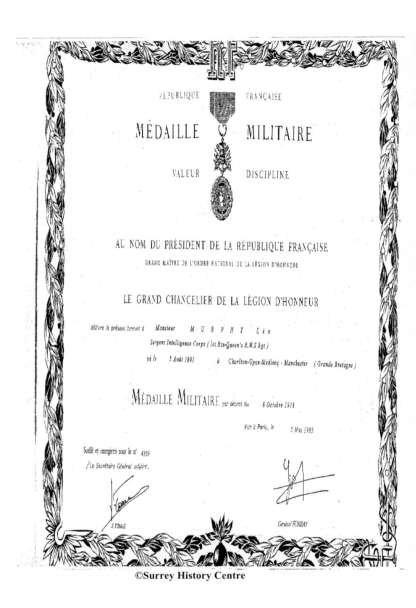

RÉPUBLIQUE FRANÇAISE

MÉDAILLE MILITAIRE

VALEUR DISCIPLINE

AU NOM DU PRÉSIDENT DE LA RÉPUBLIQUE FRANÇAISE

GRAND MAÎTRE DE L'ORDRE NATIONAL DE LA LÉGION D'HONNEUR

LE GRAND CHANCELIER DE LA LÉGION D'HONNEUR

délivre le présent brevet à Monsieur M U R P H T Léo

Sergent Intelligence Corps (1st Btn-Queen's R.W.S Rgt)

né le 5 Août 1891 à Chorlton-Upon-Medlocq - Manchester (Grande Bretagne)

MÉDAILLE MILITAIRE, par décret du 8 Octobre 1918

Fait à Paris, le 5 Mai 1995

Scellé et enregistré sous le n° 4369

/ Le Secrétaire Général adjoint,

J. TOMAS

Général FORRAY

©Surrey History Centre

RÉPUBLIQUE FRANÇAISE

Guerre 1914-1918

CITATION

EXTRAIT DE L'ORDRE GÉNÉRAL N° 382

Le Général de Division de LAGUICHE, Chef de la Mission Militaire Française, Direction d'Etapes de la Zone Britannique cite

à l'ordre de la Brigade

M U R P H Y (Jas. Norbury - N° 1/17757 A/Corporal - Royal Fusiliers, and/Intelligence Corps (précédemment 1st Bn. E. Wott Surrey Regt.).

"Les 11 et 12 Avril 1918, à la gare de BETHUNE où se trouvaient de nombreux habitants partant devant le bombardement, a fait preuve de sang-froid et d'initiative en empêchant le départ des habitants, alors que l'ennemi bombardait les environs de la gare."

CES CITATIONS COMPORTENT L'ATTRIBUTION DE LA CROIX DE GUERRE 1914-1918 AVEC ETOILE DE BRONZE

Au Q.G., le 24 Août 1918
Signé / LAGUICHE

EXTRAIT CERTIFIÉ CONFORME -
Pau, le 16 Mars 1934
Le Lt Colonel SOUBY-LAVERGNE
Commandant le Bureau central
d'archives administratives militaires

©Surrey History Centre

Leo meeting with first Earl of Ypres, John French, and Sir William Pulteney, VIP visitors to the Ypres Salient Museum in 1927.

Leo with the Ypres Mayor and Police Chief.

©Andrew Edwards

Gheluvelt Chateau in 1917 (on a display board outside Gheluvelt Church.)

©Andrew Edwards

Gheluvelt Chateau in 2019.

The Bethune Belfry in 2019.

Bethune Railway Station.

©Andrew Thornton

Cut price tickets available!

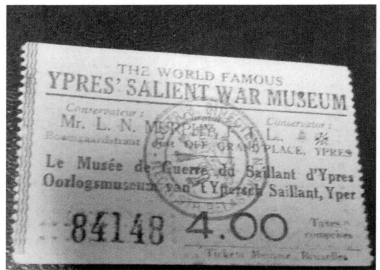

Ticket for Leo's museum in Ypres.

Saturday to Monday.

1937

WEEK-END VISIT to BELGIUM FOR TWO POUNDS

PASSPORTS ARE NOT REQUIRED, PRICE IS INCLUSIVE ! !

ANY WEEK-END WHEN NIGHT BOATS CROSS

MAKE UP YOUR PARTIES NOW ! ! (PAY SO MUCH A WEEK)

SATURDAY—

Leave Victoria at 10 p.m. (London) for Dover and Boat to OSTEND, arriving about 5-30 a.m. Sunday.

SUNDAY—

Breakfast in Ostend, then by MOTOR-COACH we visit, via the Belgium Coast, MIDDELKERKE-BAINS, WESTENDE-BAINS, NIEUPORT, seeing all the Memorials to British and Belgians on the way, FURNES, which was the G.H.Q. of ALBERT the 1st, King of the Belgians, on to HOOGSTADE, 'OOSTVLETEREN, on through the well-known ELVERDINGHE AND BRIELEN, to the famous CITY of YPRES. Here we visit the glorious MENIN GATE, THE CATHEDRAL of ST. MARTIN, with the ROSE-WINDOW given by the BRITISH ARMY and ROYAL AIR FORCE, in memory of KING ALBERT 1st, to YPRES CATHEDRAL. Then we visit THE WORLD FAMOUS "YPRES' SALIENT WAR MUSEUM," in which all branches of the various Armies are represented. This MUSEUM was completed in 1937. Then to LUNCH in "H.Q. HOTEL," in the Grand 'Place, facing the CLOTH HALL.

We spend FOUR HOURS for sightseeing and shopping in YPRES, then via THE YZER-CANAL (again by Motor Coach) to DUHALLOW (British Cemetery) "Essex Farm." Visit the well known "BRIDGE FOUR," BARD COTTAGE (all the British Cemeteries are wonderful GARDENS), then through BOISINGHE, cross the YZER to Lizerin and STEENSTRAAT, see Memorials to those gassed in the Great War, then on through WOUMEN and DIXMUDE, here we stop for TEA, then to BEERST and the "BIG-GUN " (German) known as "LONG MAX" (between COUCKELAIRE and the Village of MOERE); then through GHISTEILE and on to DINNER in OSTEND. Here we spend the evening until the BOAT leaves on MONDAY at 1 a.m. for Dover and train from DOVER arrives in (Victoria) LONDON, at 7-35 a.m. on Monday morning.

THE TWO POUNDS PAYS FOR EVERYTHING (not drinks) LONDON and RETURN, ALL MEALS, TRAIN, BOAT, MOTOR COACHES, all TOURS and TIPS.

BOOK YOUR DATE WELL IN ADVANCE, IF POSSIBLE !

FOR ANY OTHER TOURS—JUST SAY WHAT YOU REQUIRE AND WE WILL QUOTE !

Secretaries or Organisers SHOULD WRITE DIRECT TO:—

MR. L. N. MURPHY, F.I.L.,

Organiser of Official "Mons Pilgrimage," etc.

President Ypres Branch of the "Old Contemptibles' Association."

Founder and Curator of the "Ypres Salient War Museum" at Ypres.

Late of "1st Queen's Royals" and Intelligence Corps "B."

THE

BRITISH TOURING - INFORMATION BUREAU,

GRAND PLACE, YPRES, BELGIUM

Telegrams: MURPHY-Ypres.   'Phone: 195 Ypres (Two lines).   Established 1919.

Postage to Belgium 2½d.

Printed by the Avian Press, Ashbourne, and Published by the Proprietors, the Executive Council, Old Contemptibles' Association

**Advert and itinerary for one of Leo's
trips to the battlefield.**

An Old Contemptibles' parade through Ypres.

©Cecilia Wooton

Leo's ill-fated museum in Brighton.

FIRST TIME IN ENGLAND !
THE INTERNATIONAL
WAR EXHIBITION
Incorporating the World Famous
YPRES' SALIENT
WAR MUSEUM
1, 2, 3 & 4, Gloucester Place
(Telephone House) **BRIGHTON, 1** Near the Astoria

OPEN DAILY FROM 10 a.m. to 10 p.m.
Phone: Brighton No. 4511
Curator: MR. L. N. MURPHY, F.I.L.

TICKETS 1s
H.M. Forces half price. Children 6d

Ticket for Leo's WW2 Museum in Brighton.

©Andrew Edwards

Memorial to the 2nd Worcesters in Gheluvelt.

Advertisement for Leo's electrical business.

Leo's advertisement for his wife's lace shop.

An advertisement Leo placed for setting up a chess club.

Translation:

Chess Game

All chess enthusiasts are invited to give their names to M.L.N Murphy, electrician, Grand 'Place, Ypres, or come to the friendly reunion taking place at Hotel Régina, Grand'Place, Ypres, on Wednesday 10th June at 20.00 hours. Topic of the day: talk and creation of a chess club. Enthusiasts we rely on your dedication. Beginners welcome.

Article in *The Brighton Evening Argus* on the scrapping of Leo's collection.

©Andrew Edwards

Crowds and soldiers at the Menin Gate.

©Andrew Edwards

In Flanders Field Museum.

©Andrew Edwards

Shoulder to shoulder graves.

THIS·COLUMN·MARKS·THE
BATTLEFIELD·WHERE·18,000
CANADIANS·ON·THE·BRITISH
LEFT·WITHSTOOD·THE·FIRST
GERMAN·GAS·ATTACKS·THE
22-24 APRIL 1915·2,000·FELL
AND·LIE·BURIED·NEARBY

©Andrew Edwards

Brooding Soldier memorial plaque.

©Andrew Edwards

The 'Brooding Soldier'.

©Andrew Edwards

Tyne Cot Cemetery and memorial wall.

Leo's grave in Ypres cemetery.

Newspaper Reports

Within some of the various news articles below Leo is described as an Irishman, Major, Captain, yet he was none of these. His great grandfather was from Tyrone though!

Aberdeen Press and Journal – 17 April 1928:

"In Ypres, hard by the sorrowful ruins of the ancient Cloth Hall, we met an affable gentleman rejoicing in the name of Murphy, and hailing from that distressful isle where the name is so common as to be used as a synonym for potatoes. In the interval between acting as secretary of the local Chamber of Commerce, sitting on several committees, and running a free information bureau for tourists, this energetic Irishman conducts an electricity and gas business, and has lately taken to the sale of lace as well! The fact that he has a French wife and three young children may account for his active ramifications."

An extract from an article by W.A.F. entitled "Back to the Front – A Dream Realised – and Shattered." *Sheffield Daily Telegraph* – 24 September 1929:

"When one can see hens strutting unconcernedly across the road at Hell Fire Corner it is clear that the Ypres salient is no place to look for traces of the war. As a matter of fact, visitors to the battlefields flock into a museum to get their impressions. The museum is run by an ex-officer, an Irishman, who stayed behind in 1918 and gathered the most amazing collection of war relics that any one man in the world owns and is now reaping the benefit.

Among the exhibits are some Sheffield-printed volumes of the 'Lead-swinger', a journal one of the West Riding batteries used to produce. With visitors of every nation coming in he needs all his Irish wit to smooth things out. One day this summer General von Hugel, who was in charge of the German forces in the salient from 1914 to 1916, came into the museum and rather foolishly started an argument with Major Murphy, the proprietor, on the subject of war guilt. That was before The Hague Conference, and the Major pointed out that the fact that the whole of the civilised world saw British troops still in Germany after ten years without the slightest protest showed what world opinion of the war is.

General von Hugel replied, 'But they never came into Germany fighting.'

'Oh,' said Major Murphy, 'No Britisher would ever allow a foreign soldier to enter his country without

60

fighting.'

Whereupon the German General left."

An extract from the London Day by Day column "From our London Correspondent."
Leeds Mercury – **11 March 1935:**

"... Mr Murphy, however, was no stranger, for he is already known to thousands of ex-Servicemen all over Great Britain. He is the curator of the Ypres Salient War Museum, in the Grand Place, Ypres, of which the Bishop of Willesden once said, 'Anyone visiting it will go forth and forever preach peace among nations.'"

An extract from an article reporting on the Annual Conference of The Old Contemptibles' Association, which was held in Leeds and which Chum Murphy attended in his capacity as President of the Ypres Branch. Northern Whig – 25 January 1936.

THE YPRES SALIENT WAR MUSEUM.

MR L. N. MURPHY ADDRESSES OLD CONTEMPTIBLES.

"The Old Contemptibles' Association of Northern Ireland, an organisation which is rapidly assuming a pre-eminent place as far as ex-service men in the province are concerned, was honoured last night by the visit of **Mr L. N. Murphy***, president of the Ypres Branch of the Association, and curator of the world – famous Ypres Salient War Museum.*

Mr Murphy was received by the Chairman, Mr W. G. Symms; Mr James Ritchie, hon. secretary; Captain J. Gallaher, and Captain Ellison.

Mr Murphy, in the course of his remarks, referred to the activities of the Ypres Museum, which included among its exhibits weapons of defence and offence, curios of both technical and historical interest, many records of notable actions, official war photographs, and other records of the Great War.

Mr Murphy related how he was called to France at the outbreak of the war before most of his colleagues. War was declared at 11.30 a.m. (sic) on August 4th,

1914. At 6 o'clock the next morning he received his papers, and at 8 o'clock he entrained from Southampton, eventually arriving in France by the first boat on 9th August.

Mr Murphy then described the preparation of maps for his division, and in vivid detail recounted his activities during the Mons, Aisne, and Ypres campaigns. When things became 'interesting' on the Somme he went there and took part in that famous battle. Later he transferred to the Intelligence Corps. Mr Murphy disclosed how he was 'introduced' to his wife, a Frenchwoman, when she was covered by bricks and fallen masonry, and related in lively fashion how he rescued her, and, in his own words, 'lived happily ever after'.

After further recollections of war experiences, Mr Murphy brought his talk to a close.

Leo had previously attended the second Annual Dinner of the Lichfield Branch of The Old Contemptibles' Association, held on 18th January, before going to Belfast.

He also acted as a guide to the Old Contemptibles' Association of Northern Ireland party which visited France and Flanders in August 1936. As a gesture of gratitude, the Ulster Chums presented Mrs Murphy with an Irish linen tablecloth."

Liverpool Echo – 29 July 1937:

Murphy of Manchester

*"Among the thousands of exhibits in the Ypres Salient War Museum – founded and owned by **Mr L. N. Murphy**, of 18, Lime-grove, Manchester – are the special badges given to the Liverpool Pals' Battalion, including one in solid silver given by Lord Derby to the first 100 who enlisted in the battalion. 'Sans Changer', runs the motto. Murphy, of Manchester, points it out to all the parties he conducts round this fearsome arsenal.*

He values the whole collection at two million francs (£14,000). If you care to buy it at this figure, you will be the owner of the most remarkable war museum outside Great Britain. In another case are the badges of every regiment which ever served on 'Westfront'. Part of the curator's 'stuff' is to ask if you can spot the badge of 'the finest regiment in the British Isles.' You were King's, or Pals or Liverpool Scottish, and say, 'yes'. You were South Lancashires and say 'yes'. You were Lancashire Fusiliers, and the answer's just the same. So everyone's satisfied!"

An extract from an article written by Victor Hyde M.C., entitled "A Lancashire Pilgrim in Passion Dale."

Clitherhoe Advertiser and Times, 6 August 1937:

"I paid a visit to a museum in charge of an Irishman, named Murphy, who has a Belgian and a Frenchman as assistants, and there you can see almost every memento of the war in the form of weapons and appliances – even the old rum jar, used to put spirit into you!"

An extract from an article written by J.C.D. entitled "Where They Lie in Peace: Clitheronian Visits the Old Battlefields of France."

Belfast Telegraph – 20th August 1938:

MEMORIAL AT YPRES.

UNVEILING NEXT SUNDAY.

ULSTER OLD CONTEMPTIBLES.

"A party of 70 Old Contemptibles from Ulster arrived in London to-day on the way to Ypres, Belgium, where a tablet will be unveiled on Sunday by the Mayor of Ypres.

Included in the party are **Mr L. N. Murphy**, vice-president North Ireland Old Contemptibles' Association; Major Nolan, Major Donnelly, and Mr Richie, organising hon. secretary Northern Ireland.

The wording of the tablet is as follows:

'To the glory of God and in immortal memory of all ranks of the contemptible little British Army who fought around Ypres and in the Salient during those critical days, October 11 – November 22, 1914, and in remembrance of those of that army who fell by the way.
Erected by the Old Contemptibles' Association of Northern Ireland, August 21, 1938.'

The party will spend two days in Ypres and two days in Brussels. An official reception will be given in their honour at Mons by the Mayor on the anniversary of the first Battle of Mons, August 23. They will return to Ypres for a tour of the battlefields and leave for Belfast on Sunday week."

67

A report on the 1938 pilgrimage of The Old Contemptibles' Association of Northern Ireland published in *The Northern Whig* on 20th August, included the following paragraph:

"The men are looking forward to meeting again Major L. N. Murphy, an Irishman and member of the Association, who is in Ypres. He holds the French Croix de Guerre and the Medal Militaire (sic), and was attached to the Army Intelligence Corps. Major Murphy acts as interpreter and is very popular."

Scunthorpe Evening Telegraph — 6 September 1939:

"Mr Murphy, founder and owner of the Ypres Salient War Museum, has received instructions from the Belgian authorities to be ready to evacuate and hand over the building within 24 hours. He is thinking of bringing his collection to England."

Cambridge Daily News – **7 December 1939:**

FROM YPRES TO LONDON?

"Over in Ypres is an exhibition of a different kind. It is a museum of historic and other relics of the last war, to which the armies of all the combatants contributed.

The present war endows it with exceptional interest. But Ypres is, by reason of the war, not so accessible as it was; moreover, strange as it may strike one at first thought, Ypres is a neutral territory. It is in Belgium, and is not one of those old war centres within reach of our soldiers in the West.

But thousands of soldiers could see this collection if it were brought to England. And that is what may happen.

*The founder and curator of the Ypres Salient War Museum, **Mr L. N. Murphy**, says that his wonderful show may be visiting these shores shortly. It is not an easy move to arrange, but it is the tradition of Ypres never to be defeated."*

Credits

Cyrille Le Roux: A former colleague who helped identify Leo for me.

Andrew Thornton: Military Historian who researched Leo for me and supplied most of the press articles and adverts. Andrew is the leading expert on the Old Contemptibles.

Surrey History Centre – Provided documents from Francis Murphy.

Francis Murphy: Leo's eldest son who deposited Leo's citations together with a biography of his father with The Queens Surrey Regimental Museum (now held in Surrey County Archives)

Dominiek Dendooven: from Ypres (in Flanders Field Museum), who provided a wealth of information held by the museum.

Shrewsbury Library Writers Lab for their advice and fantastic support.

Susan Livings and Cecilia Wootton: Leo's granddaughters for their memories, photographs and supporting and encouraging me. Cecilia also proved to be an excellent proofreader!

Helen Edwards: Who provided support and advice and who assisted me in self-publishing Leo's story.

About the author

Andrew Edwards is a retired businessman who has had a lifetime's interest in WW1 ever since his grandad, Joseph Edwards, sat him on his knee and related tales from the war. One anecdote was about being bayonetted in the leg by a German soldier during the Battle of the Somme: "Best birthday present I ever had as I got sent home and never returned."

Andrew has made numerous visits to the Battlefields of Belgium and Northern France and plans to present Leo's story to various organisations in 2023.

Contact Details:

Email: andrew.r.edwards@btinternet.com

Printed in Great Britain
by Amazon

14286646R00047